For Cindy---

An incredibly PINK woman

The Little Book of PINK

*Affirmations and Quotations for
Healing and High Vibrations*

Rena M. Reese

ISBN: 1434838382
EAN 13: 9781434838384
Printed in the USA

www.MySoulSalon.com

© 2008 Rena M. Reese
All Rights Reserved

Related titles also by Rena Reese:

Journey Like a Shaman!
Audio CD & Meditation Journal

The Soul Salon

Streaking for the Soul

"Although we wish for the wind to be at our back in life, it is when the wind is at our face and whips in resistance, that our kite soars."

----Rena Reese

The Little Book of PINK

Our Nature

The human body, the human spirit, and The Divine, all work together to choreograph our human experience.

One of these three elements of our nature, *The Divine*, is a constant source of love, unwavering strength and purity. When our human body or spirit meets with a challenge, God, who is part of our nature, is an abundant source of comfort and positive power.

God lives in us. Since we were created in His Image and Likeness, all that we know to be true about Him has a place in us. All that is magical, powerful and abundant about The Divine has been shared with us. He told us so.

God is love,
> power,
> compassion,
> and healing.

He is light,
> hope,
> unbounded potential,
> and infinite possibility.

Each of us enjoys these same characteristics contained in every strand of our spiritual and physical DNA. Own this truth as you make choices, heal your body and create your life.

The Little Book of PINK

When it comes to your physical and spiritual well being, your **thoughts** matter. The **company you keep** matters. The **foods you eat**, the **conversations you have**, the **words you speak and read**, ALL matter. Allow your Divine-nature to blanket all of your choices. In doing so, you will raise the vibration of your body and make choices that beam with self-advocacy. You will be an inspiration to others, a beacon of light, and full of life and vibrancy. Imagine if everyone did this. What a happy, healthy, high vibration world we would live in.

If healthy and happy were to be represented as a color, pink seems a logical choice. Not that red, orange and green are not great colors, but the color

The Little Book of PINK

of bubble gum and rosy cheeks seems to exude a happy pink-ness. Let the color pink remind you to let the quest for high vibrations, bliss and abundant health to be woven through all that you do each day.

Be Pink.

The Little Book of PINK

Pink Affirmations

Affirmations are used as a tool to focus your thoughts. The value comes when you allow the words to really percolate in your mind and heart. Intentionally filling your consciousness with positive content, you will edge out negativity.

It is natural when facing health challenges or an emotionally draining circumstance to have thoughts that don't serve you positively. When you recognize these thoughts, you can silence them by consciously replacing them. Replacing that negative seed with a positive mantra or thought can alter your mood, vision and your physical state. Each of these contributes to the creation of what you would like to manifest in your life.

Your thoughts are powerful and they exert that power without ceasing in every waking moment. Use them to create what you desire.

The Little Book of PINK

Pink Affirmations

My body is a divinely created piece of art. Crafted by the ultimate creator, it is infused with unbounded Divine intelligence. I can tap into this wisdom and know exactly what my body needs to thrive and heal.

The Little Book of PINK

My Divine spirit speaks to each cell of my body and every strand of my DNA. My cells listen attentively and respond by thriving. I absorb the purest energy, abundant love and healing light from the universe.

The Little Book of PINK

I make loving choices wrapped in self-care. I choose to think positive thoughts and surround myself with positive people.

The Little Book of PINK

Should I feel that I need a dose of Divine light and love, it is always available to me. I only need to close my eyes and visualize the beam of light and love coming directly to me from the heavens. It is funneled directly from its source, the source of all things, God.

I receive it directly through the top of my head and my body drinks it up until I am full. I glow, full of Divine love and light. I am filled up to the top of my head, my crown. I am satisfied, renewed, energized and tingly.

The Little Book of PINK

I am blanketed with pure and pristine healing energy. Only positive thoughts and powerful mantras flow through me and speak to my cells.

All is well. I am breathing in Divine healing-energy and light. I exhale any impurities in my body, organs, blood or flesh. My body only welcomes and sustains high vibration cells. They multiply and produce more healthy high vibration cells. I am buzzing with the vibrations of my healthy, happy cells.

The Little Book of PINK

I trust the wisdom that my body holds. It knows exactly what I need to thrive. I hear the whispers of my spirit and I honor them. I make choices that show respect for the Divine-me. I am supremely connected to my Source and I live IN the light.

I do not need to know all the answers. I openly receive the Grace of God even as I wonder about certain mysteries of life. Although I may wonder "Why?" it is not required that I understand all things. The empty place that leaves me wanting to know the answers to life's mysteries is somehow full and not really empty at all. It is filled with trust and knowing that all is well.

The Little Book of PINK

I am a powerful human being. I govern my thoughts. I choose positive thoughts and embody their messages.

I choose to be a vibrant presence here on the planet. My light beams from each pore of my body. I am a light queen, filled with the pure, white light.

The Little Book of PINK

It is my responsibility to care for my spirit and body. I have been entrusted with the care of each of these by my creator, God. I will honor the trust placed in me by Him. I will do this by truly hearing when my body speaks to me. My intuition and my body send me messages that only I can interpret and honor. I am supremely connected to them both.

The Little Book of PINK

Each day is charged with possibility, healing and energy. It is my job to show up, ready to receive these things and then share my high vibration with the planet. I am a source of light because I allow the Divine light of God to flow *to* and *through* me.

The Little Book of PINK

My happiness absolutely matters. When I take good care of myself I am a vibrant presence to those who share my world. My vibrancy and bliss shines out to all people. It is self-less to take care of me. I embrace and accept this sacred responsibility.

The Little Book of PINK

The world can benefit from my light. When I care for my needs, I contribute a "high-vibration me" to the world. This is a hugely wonderful gift to the planet and to me. If I am sick or sad, that will never contribute wellness and joy to others. It is in lobbying for my healthiest and happiest life, that I share my light.

The Little Book of PINK

There are things that I can do that no one can do in the same way. I celebrate my gifts and skills and encourage others to do the same. A world where everyone owns their greatness and celebrates what they can contribute to others is a high vibration world. I am gifted. We are all gifted.

The Little Book of PINK

Every cell of my body is vibrant. Each cell has a Divine intelligence that communicates with me. I know when I need to rest, socialize, meditate, commune with nature and nourish myself. This is a priority for me because it is my responsibility to advocate for my health and wellness.

It is a sacred, Divine and spiritual responsibility to care for myself in this manner and I do it joyfully. When I do this, it gives others permission to do the same. I act in a spiritually responsible manner when I take care of me.

The Little Book of PINK

I have faith that all is well. Although there are times I face challenges, I am fully capable of approaching them and dealing with them. I take responsibility for my choices and know I am creating my life. When I cannot change an event, I choose to positively govern my reactions to that event. I am powerful. I am decisive. I am patient.

The Little Book of PINK

There is a gift in my blunders. I accept that gift with gratitude. I release myself from any guilt that I have carried with me. I am here to learn. I am here to feel and experience a range of emotions so that I can grow. I can release any guilt I feel for choices I am not proud of. I can release any guilt I feel for hurting another human being. I choose to release the expectation I have placed on myself to be infallible. I choose to replace guilt with gratitude for being smarter, more compassionate and human.

The Little Book of PINK

Happiness is my natural state. My spirit craves joy, connection, and alignment. I gravitate to people, events and places that support my spirit being in a happy place. I magnetize these people to me. I magnetize these events to me. I am a bliss magnet. Happiness gently vibrates my cells all the way to abundant health.

The Little Book of PINK

My physical body is what is seen by the world. I know that my spiritual world is infinitely more real and powerful than the physical. I can choose to allow or repel anything in my physical experience. I am in charge. I am the gatekeeper.

The Little Book of PINK

Much like an energetic suit of armor, my aura is my spiritual skin. I can pull it in close to my body when I feel the need to do so. I can let it out to expand when I feel I am in a pure and divine space. When I feel I could use the gift of God's healing and love, I invite His Divine light to shine down on me. I welcome the light through the top of my head and allow it to fill me and my aura like helium fills a balloon. This love and light is always available to me.

The Little Book of PINK

My hands are capable of receiving and giving. I trust my Divine intelligence to signal me when it is time to give. I will also trust that I will know when it is time to receive. This is the way of life. This is the nature of things and so it must be honored. Today I will know if it is in my best interest to give or receive.

The Little Book of PINK

There is a child in me. I hear her speak to me and tell me what she needs. I instinctively know how to fill that need. I know how to offer the nurturing support and help required so that the child in me will thrive. I know how to offer nurturing and forgiveness.

I hear the voice of the child that lives in me. Her whispers will always lead me to a place of healing and self-care.

The Little Book of PINK

I have much to be grateful for. I have unbridled gratitude for certain people in my life. They feel my appreciation and love. When I think of these lovely people a smile stretches across my face. I feel so loved and so very lucky.

The Little Book of PINK

I choose to thank my body. I appreciate my body's ability to maintain balance and a clean, healthy energy. My body is like an instrument that requires tuning. I provide it with the time and space it needs to align, refresh and rejuvenate.

The Little Book of PINK

I am an artist. I design my life. If I do not like what I have brushed upon my canvas, I can choose to paint a new reality. In just deciding I want something to be different, I can manifest these changes. My life, my canvas, is under my creative control. I can create anything I decide is important to my spirit.

The Little Book of PINK

I am a conduit of Divine energy. This energy is the source of all. It is light, love and unbounded power. I can call upon this energy anytime at all and know it will infuse me with the strength and guidance I may need.

The Little Book of PINK

I embrace the good things that life has to offer. I celebrate and enjoy the richness of life. There is a buffet of wonderful-ness for me to partake in. I choose to enjoy it all because it was created for this purpose. I honor God by enjoying His gifts.

The Little Book of PINK

I allow my spirit to enjoy solitude when it needs it. Alone time is not a luxury; it is a responsibility. Solitude heals, births creative thought, and connects me with God. There is a time to focus on my inner life and inner world. I allow this time to serve me for my maximum benefit.

My intuition is God in me. I honor this voice even when it makes no sense or seems hard. I know that my intuition tells me what I need to thrive and heal. My intuition is the Divine in me and therefore it will never lead me astray.

The Little Book of PINK

My spirit animates my body. Even at rest, I am lively, healthy, and sparkling. My cells are like zillions of diamonds that have come together to form my physical-self.

The Little Book of PINK

I am open to the lessons presented to me on my spiritual path. My lessons are unique to me and designed just for me. I easily grasp the lessons as they are presented to me.

I am so grateful for my human experience. It is this experience that fosters the richness of my physical and spiritual experience.

The Little Book of PINK

I am resourceful. I am instinctively able to design healthy, appropriate responses to a situation. I have everything I need within me to handle adversity.

The Little Book of PINK

All is one. I know this is true so I cannot view myself as apart from another. I choose to be benevolent toward all. I choose to offer compassion to all. Since this is my way of being, I receive compassion and goodness too. This is because all is one.

The Little Book of PINK

No one can take advantage of me without my permission. I do not give this permission to anyone, ever. I give of my time and energy when it feeds my spirit. I give with no strings attached. When I say yes, I say yes with 100% of myself, or I will say no.

The Little Book of PINK

I am in control and empowered. I own this power even if it feels uncomfortable at times. If I am not the one making the choices in my life, I am allowing something else to design my world.

I am the creator of my experience and I can make courageous choices, even if it feels difficult. I am pretty darn powerful and I can own my power and embrace change.

The Little Book of PINK

I can serve without being a slave. I can offer my gifts and make a contribution to the world in a way that elevates my spirit and raises my vibration. I choose to give when I am authentically joyful to do so. This makes my gift pure.

The Little Book of PINK

I can count on myself. I feel the nudges of my spirit and I honor them. I hear the whispers of my soul and act on them. I ultimately know what sustains me and I choose those things.

The Little Book of PINK

I seek truth. I insist on honoring my truth.

I courageously acknowledge what is truth for me even if it will not be easy to act on. I may want things to be different, but I can see them as they really are. When I honestly name my truth, I am better able to choose what I need, the people I want in my life and the things I will do each day. Truth will lead me to my happiest, healthiest self.

The Little Book of PINK

I delight in offering acts of love to others. This delight is its own reward. I feel so satisfied to know that I have eased a burden, given support, or offered a kind word. The high vibration of my gift cycles back around to me and elevates me too. How delightful.

The Little Book of PINK

I am in constant union with the Divine. I know this is true because I have consciously welcomed this relationship into my life. My Divine connection is intimate, light-filled, pure and healing. I am so grateful for this mystic alliance.

The Little Book of PINK

I welcome energizing, positive thoughts into my awareness. When something is less than positive I quickly catch it and reframe it, so that it suits the vision I have for my life. The more I do this, the more that it becomes my natural state. I am a positive light-filled being that resonates with all that has a high vibration.

The Little Book of PINK

I spend time envisioning what I want to create in my life. I can see in great detail the beautiful life that is mine. I can envision my personal connections and my environment. I can achieve anything that I can visualize. Spending time with my visualizations will help them manifest!

The Little Book of PINK

I am at ease with the presence of angels in my life. I enjoy angel love when I am both happy and in need of support. I accept the form that the angel love enters my life. It is spontaneous and wonderful. All angel love is a gift that I openly look for and invite into my daily existence.

The Little Book of PINK

I intuitively know just what I need to support my healthiest body and happiest life. I make these choices proudly and without apology. My intuition is a tool I use responsibly. It aligns me with the Divine. I can repair my body with the use of my intuition. I can transform my mind and spirit with the power of my intuition. I take care of myself.

The Little Book of PINK

I am willing to look at my life with fresh eyes. I know that progress comes from courageously assessing what is truth. A new perspective can birth new goals. I welcome both of these into my life.

The Little Book of PINK

There is beauty in all things. This beauty is sacred because it emanates from God. I am part of this beauty and I accept the sacred part of me.

The Little Book of PINK

I keep my power as I handle what comes up in my life. I am strong, willing and able to traverse the road I am on. My body is up for the task; my heart is dedicated to my spirit's quest. I am on my mark like an Olympian. I choose to create healthy cells. I choose to have a peaceful demeanor. I choose a life of harmony.

The Little Book of PINK

I am willing to re-work and change anything that I know is not working for my greatest good. I am supremely connected to all that fills my days and I choose each thing intentionally.

I know the people I need around me. I know the physical environment that is peaceful and healing and the thoughts that must fill me head. I choose only that which works toward my greatest good.

The Little Book of PINK

I embrace what comes to me with joy and love. I may not understand all that comes my way; I accept the gift and release any sadness. I trust that I am learning what I came here to learn. I will grasp the lesson and release the experience with gratitude. I am through with it now.

The Little Book of PINK

I can express who I am and what I truly feel. I am free. I am peaceful. I nourish my body and spirit with what it needs to thrive. This nourishment comes from living happily and with love. This is my natural state and I choose it now.

The Little Book of PINK

It is my choice to live in a joyous state. I give forgiveness where it is needed so that I can be done with the past. I release the past to the place it belongs. I invest 100% of my energy in living in the present moment. I choose joy, love, and peace as a way of being.

The Little Book of PINK

I allow life to nourish me with what I need. I allow the Divine to provide me with the sustenance I thrive on. I allow this nourishment and take it in easily.

The Little Book of PINK

I am a wonderful creation. My body is amazing. I trust my body has a Divine intelligence programmed into every cell. It can heal, thrive and serve my needs.

The Little Book of PINK

I am relaxing into the truth that I am safe. I am at peace knowing I am protected, loved and truly supported in all things great and small.

The Little Book of PINK

I choose life.
I am life.
I love life.

The Little Book of PINK

I can create things just as I want them to be. I can create anything by spending time with my thoughts. I can visualize my way to abundant health and ease. I can see it in my mind's eye. I believe it is possible because I can create it in my mind. My mind communicates with the Divine energy of the Universe to manifest whatever I desire. I desire a vibrant life and healthy body.

The Little Book of PINK

I approve of myself. I love myself as I am today. I appreciate my ability to learn, grow and change. I am willing to do each of these. I am willing to learn. I am willing to grow. I am willing to change.

Amazingly I am perfectly wonderful, even as I learn, grow, and change.

The Little Book of PINK

I am allowing goodness, healing and love to flow to me. I deserve goodness. I deserve healing. I deserve love. I allow all good things to enter my experience.

The Little Book of PINK

I slow down when my body signals me to rest. I seek quiet when my spirit needs peace. I hear and honor the signals my body and spirit send me. I am rewarded with a content and vibrant spirit as well as a healthy body.

The Little Book of PINK

I joyfully express gratitude and appreciation. I choose to live in gratitude. This state magnetizes more of what I am grateful for.

The Little Book of PINK

I know what is a priority for me. I know what my spirit craves. I know what my body needs to thrive. My intuition guides me with perfect accuracy, so that I can act out of self-love.

The Little Book of PINK

My spirit is infused with a Divine intelligence. I am constantly nudged toward what energizes me. I am nudged away from what depletes me. I choose to honor the nudges of my spirit. My intuition is a powerful tool. I use it to create a healthy spirit, healthy body and healthy life.

The Little Book of PINK

I make time to indulge in activities that are pleasing to me. I make time to enjoy nature, hear my spirit and rest. I choose to advocate for a happy, healthy me.

The Little Book of PINK

I find ways to express my creative energy in my life. I am the creator of my life, my body, and my home. I accept creative control over each of these.

The Little Book of PINK

I have gifts to contribute to the world. I choose to acknowledge these gifts and share them. I am kind, loving and gifted in many ways.

The Little Book of PINK

I choose to live authentically as the "real" me. No one is better qualified to do this than I am. I will allow my spirit to vote on what it needs. The judgments of others have no place in creating my life. I answer to my Divine-self, my spirit.

The Little Book of PINK

Creating your Own Affirmations

As you read, a mantra, affirmation or desired way of being may pop into your head. Write each of these down as they come up on the pages provided here. You will create a valuable anthology of your growth, healing and evolution of power.

The Little Book of PINK

My Own Affirmations...

The Little Book of PINK

My Own Affirmations...

The Little Book of PINK

Pink Quotes

"The wish for healing has ever been the half of health."

"Nothing...refreshes and aids a sick man so much as the affection of his friends."

---Seneca the Younger
(~5B.C.-A.D.65)

The Little Book of PINK

"Patient, heal thyself."
>---Doctor's Saying

"Rise and go your way;
your faith has made you well."

>---Jesus
>Reply to a Samaritan who had thrown himself at the feet of Jesus in gratitude for his healing.

"In health the flesh is graced, the holy enters the world."

>---Wendell Berry
>What are People for?: Essays

The Little Book of PINK

"Thy self is the master of thyself, and thy Self is thy refuge."

---The Dhammapada: The Path of Perfection

"We feel safe, huddled within human institutions—churches, banks, madrigal groups—but these concoctions melt away at the basic moment. The self's responsibility, then, is to achieve rapport if not rapture with the giant, cosmic other: to appreciate, let's say, the walk back from the mailbox."

---John Updike
Self-Consciousness: Memoirs

The Little Book of PINK

"Inner space is the real frontier."

---Gloria Steinem

"I have felt his hands upon me in great trials and submitted to His guidance, and I trust that as He shall further open the way, I will be ready to walk therein, relying on His help and trusting in His goodness and wisdom."

---Abraham Lincoln

The Little Book of PINK

"Faith is nothing but a living, wide-awake consciousness of God within."

"Faith does not contradict reason but transcends it."

---Mohandas K. Gandhi

"All dis-ease comes from a state of un-forgiveness. Whenever we are ill, we need to search our hearts to see who it is we need to forgive."

---Louise Hay
You Can Heal Your Life

The Little Book of PINK

"Although the world is full of suffering, it is also full of the overcoming of it.

---Helen Keller

"It is in your moments of decision that your destiny is shaped."

---Anthony Robbins

"Out of difficulties grow miracles."

---Jean de La Bruyere

"Be courageous! Have faith! Go forward."

---Thomas Edison

The Little Book of PINK

"There is a giant asleep within every man. When the giant awakes, miracles happen."

---Frederick Faust

"Nobody cares if you can't dance well. Just get up and dance."

---Dave Barry

"By perseverance the snail reached the ark."

---Charles Haddon Spurgeon

The Little Book of PINK

"I will love the light for it shows me the way. Yet I will endure the darkness for it shows me the stars."

---Og Mandino

"What saves a man is to take a step. Then another step."

---Antoine De Saint-Exupery

"The person who moves a mountain begins by carrying away small stones."

---Chinese Proverb

"Expect a miracle."

---Oral Roberts

"There are two days in the week about which and upon I do not worry... One of these days is Yesterday... And the other day I do not worry about is Tomorrow.

---Robert Jones Burdette

"Hope, the best comfort of our imperfect condition.

---Edward Gibson

"Angels fly because they take themselves lightly."

---G.K. Chesterson

The Little Book of PINK

My Personal Pink Notes

The Little Book of PINK

My Personal Pink Notes

The Little Book of PINK

My Personal Pink Notes

The Little Book of PINK

My Personal Pink Notes

The Little Book of PINK

My Personal Pink Notes

The Little Book of PINK

Please visit

www.MySoulSalon.com

for additional books, tools and information on living a healthy, high vibration life.

Made in the USA
Coppell, TX
05 December 2019